INDIA

Written by Sadie Hallworth

PowerKiDS
press

Published in 2025
by The Rosen Publishing Group, Inc.
2544 Clinton Street, Buffalo, NY 14224

© 2024 BookLife Publishing Ltd.

Written by: Sadie Hallworth
Edited by: Elise Carraway
Designed by: Ker Ker Lee

Cataloging-in-Publication Data

Names: Hallworth, Sadie.
Title: India / Sadie Hallworth.
Description: Buffalo, NY : PowerKids Press, 2025. | Series: Countries of the world | Includes glossary and index.
Identifiers: ISBN 9781499449228 (pbk.) | ISBN 9781499449235 (library bound) | ISBN 9781499449242 (ebook)
Subjects: LCSH: India--Juvenile literature. | India--History--Juvenile literature.
Classification: LCC DS407.H355 2025 | DDC 954--dc23

Manufactured in the United States of America
CPSIA Compliance Information: Batch #CW25PK. For further information contact Rosen Publishing at 1-800-237-9932.

Find us on  

Image Credits

All images are courtesy of Shutterstock.com, unless otherwise specified. With thanks to Getty Images, Thinkstock Photo and iStockphoto. Cover – Anna Kosheleva, GoodStudio, Roop_Dey, PRASANNAPIX, Ravsky. 2–3 – Don Mammoser. 4–5 – NareshSharma, Andrei Minsk. 6–7 – karthi_munirathinam, Kurkul, PradeepGaurs. 8–9 – StockImageFactory.com, Toa55. 10–11 – paul prescott, Stock Exchange. 12–13 – Roop_Dey, Maythee Voran, WESTOCK PRODUCTIONS. 14–15 – Paulose NK, Snehal Jeevan Pailkar. 16–17 – Dmitry Kalinovsky, IndianFaces. 18–19 – Shahjehan, Stefano Embe. 20–21 – Indian Creations, Pixel-Shot, mae_chaba. 22–23 – Gayamal Rathnavibushana, Nicoleta Ionescu.

CONTENTS

Words that look like <u>this</u> can be found in the glossary on page 24.

WHERE IS INDIA?

India is a large country in the southern part of Asia. India is between China and Pakistan.

The capital city of India is New Delhi. India has many official languages, including Hindi, English, and 20 more.

LANDSCAPE AND WEATHER

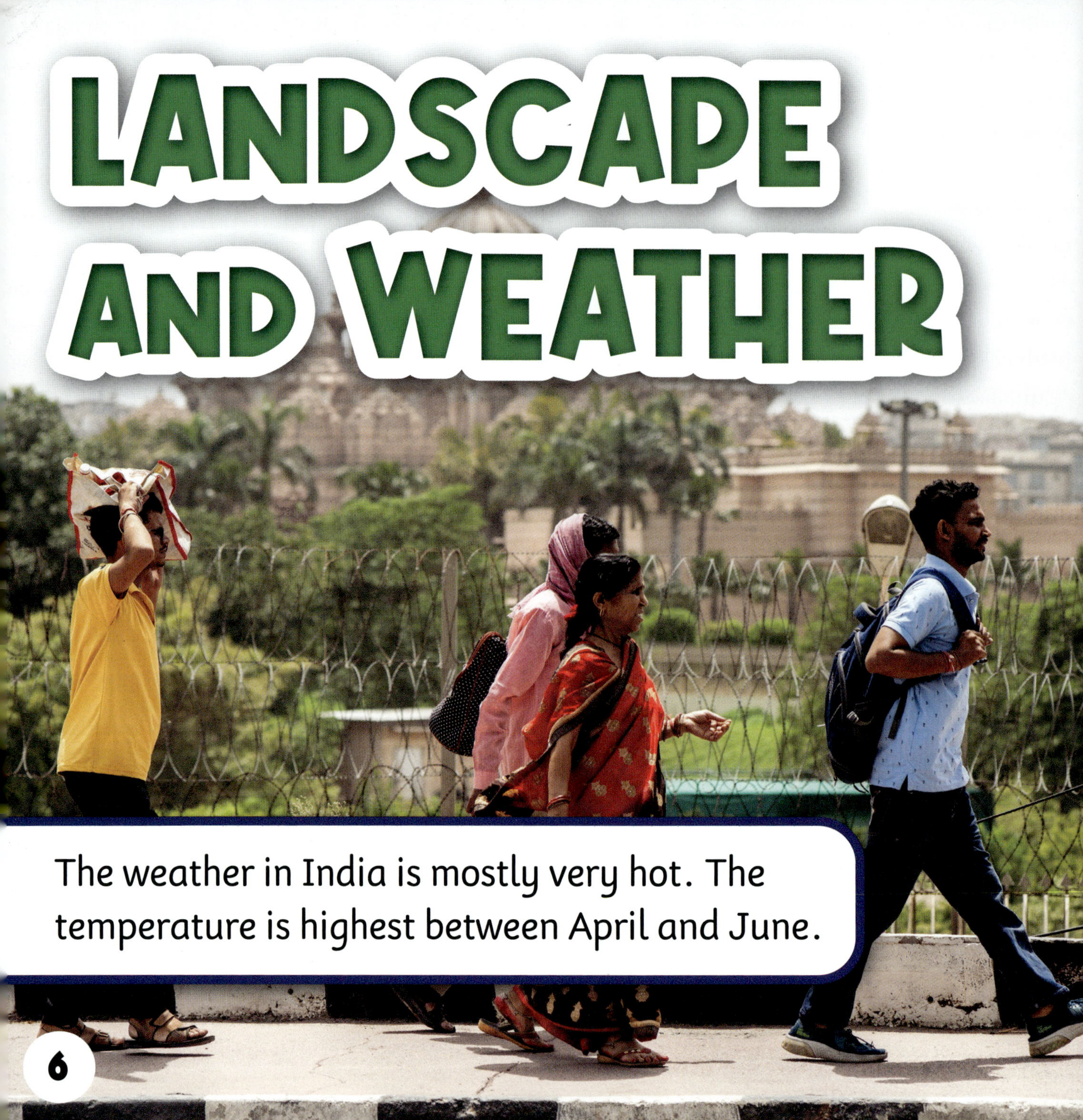

The weather in India is mostly very hot. The temperature is highest between April and June.

India has many different landscapes. Some parts of the country have mountains and rivers, and other parts are next to the sea.

RELIGION

The most-followed <u>religion</u> in India is Hinduism. There are also many other religions that are followed in India, including Islam, Christianity, Sikhism, and Buddhism.

During the Hindu festival of Diwali, people celebrate by decorating their homes with lamps, giving gifts, and eating together with their families.

FAMILIES

Indian families <u>traditionally</u> live in the same house. Grandparents, parents, aunts, uncles, and children can all live together.

Family members
are often very
close and try to
help and support
each other.

Children in India must go to school until they are 14 years old. Indian children are taught subjects such as math, sports, and how to read and write English.

There are fewer schools in the villages compared to the number of schools in the cities.

HOME

The types of houses in the cities are very different from those in the villages. The capital of India, New Delhi, has skyscrapers and <u>modern</u> houses.

Bungalows are a popular type of house in India. Bungalows only have one floor. They often have outdoor spaces called verandas.

CLOTHING

A traditional piece of clothing for ladies in India is a sari. The sari is a piece of long material that is wrapped around the body. People wrap their sari differently depending on where they are from.

Indian men usually only wear their traditional clothing for special <u>occasions</u>. For some Indian men, part of their traditional dress is a long piece of material wrapped around the head. This is called a turban.

SPORTS

The most popular sport in India is cricket. The Indian Premier League for cricket is held in India every year.

Many other sports are also popular in India, including soccer and field hockey.

FOOD

Curry is thought of as one of the most popular dishes in India. Indian food is known for having lots of different herbs and spices.

Food, such as bread, is traditionally eaten using just the right hand. The bread is torn into pieces and used to scoop food like a spoon.

21

FUN FACTS

India is home to the largest <u>population</u> of Bengal tigers in the world.

Bollywood is the Indian film industry. Bollywood makes over 1,000 films every year.

GLOSSARY

festival	a time when people come together to celebrate a special event
industry	business
modern	to do with recent or present times
occasions	special events
official	to do with something that is recognized as having power or being important
population	the number of people or animals living in a place
religion	a system of faith and worship, especially to do with a god or gods
traditionally	to do with beliefs, customs, or ways of behaving that have been around for a long time

INDEX